T0266207

Living the Good News
    a division of Church Publishing Incorporated
Editorial Offices
600 Grant Street, Suite 630
Denver, CO 80203

Cover Photograph: Regan MacStravic
Illustrations: Susan Chapman

The scripture quotations used herein are from *The New Oxford Annotated Bible with the Apocrypha, Revised Standard Version.* © 1973, 1977 by Oxford University Press. Used by permission.

Excerpts from *The Book of Common Prayer*, published by Church Publishing Corporation, 1979.

ISBN: 978-1-9319-6037-3

Everyone who has been baptized into the Christian family is invited to share Holy Communion with one another and with Jesus. Baptism makes you part of this extended family and makes you welcome at the Eucharist, the special, sacred family meal.

My name, given to me at Baptism, is

_____

I was baptized and made part of the Christian family

on (date) _____

at (church) _____

Draw or paste a recent picture of yourself here. Sign your name underneath.

This is me, now.

_____

Signature

This Bread & This Cup

by Mary Lee Wile

Table of Contents

1 Companionship:
Sharing a Meal

Draw a picture of Thanksgiving dinner. What foods go on the table? Draw them. (If you like, you can write about Thanksgiving instead.)

What else is on the table? Are there plates and glasses? Are there candles or flowers or napkins? Draw those things, too.

What people gather for Thanksgiving dinner? Draw them around the table.

The word "Eucharist" comes from a Greek word in the Bible. It means giving thanks. Jesus made Eucharist when he took bread and gave thanks to God. In church, we take bread and give thanks to God, too. Our Eucharist is a special kind of Thanksgiving meal we share with the whole Christian family.

The altar is a special kind of table for the Eucharist. Draw the bread and wine we see on the altar. What else might be on or near the altar? Draw these things, too.

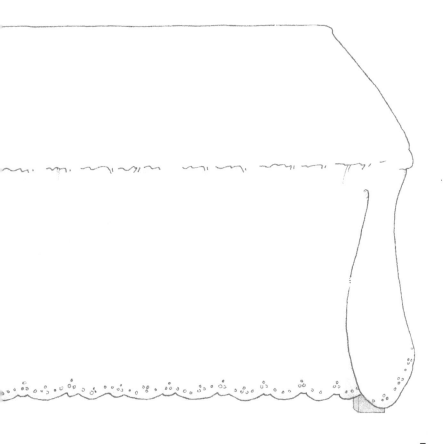

When you were baptized, you became part of a much bigger family. This is God's gift to you. God made you part of the family of Christians. We find this family not only at this church, but throughout the whole world. This family is not only those alive now but all Christians who have ever lived. Even the saints are part of your family! Even those Christians who have not yet been born are part of this new family.

When you take Communion, you are sharing a special Thanksgiving meal with the Christian family everywhere. Draw a picture of people taking Communion at your church.

Now imagine that millions and millions of people from everywhere and from all time are there with you.

Turn one of your hands upside down. Draw or trace it here.

Every time you take the bread of Communion
into your hands, you are doing what millions
of people have been doing for over 2000
years, ever since Jesus first broke bread with
his friends and family. Imagine Jesus as the
one who offers you this bread week by week.
Imagine Jesus as the one who puts the Bread
of Heaven into your outstretched hands.

Storytelling:
How the Gospel Stories Tell our Story

Once Jesus fed 5000 people with just five loaves of bread and two fish. Listen to the story from Matthew's gospel (14:13-21). Draw the bread and the fish.

That was a lot of people to feed with such a small amount of food. In the Eucharist, Jesus does even more. He feeds millions of Christians every week!

Now listen to the story of Jesus' Last Supper with his friends. Jesus blessed the bread and wine. He said he would be with his friends—and with us—whenever we share this Holy Communion. The story might sound familiar because the priest retells it every Sunday. Draw the kind of bread your church uses for Communion.

Table fellowship is gathering around a table to share a meal. Thanksgiving dinner is one kind of table fellowship your family shares.

Table fellowship was so important to Jesus that he shared meals with his friends even after his death and Resurrection. One night he walked to a town called Emmaus with some friends. At first, they didn't know who he was. He told them stories from the Bible while they walked. At their table he took and blessed and broke the bread. That's when they knew it was Jesus!

Draw a picture of Jesus holding bread.

Sometimes in church we might sing, "Be known to us, Lord Jesus, in the breaking of the bread." We get to know Jesus when we share bread at the Eucharist.

We also get to know Jesus when we share stories about him. The last story in John's gospel tells how Jesus, after his Resurrection, cooked breakfast on the beach for his friends. Listen to the story.

Besides being fed by Jesus, we are asked to feed and take care of others. Can you think of people or pets that you already help take care of? Draw or write about them here:

3 These Holy Things:
What We Use in the Eucharist

You may have toured the church with your family or group. What surprised you most as you explored the church?

VESTMENTS MEANS CLOTHES USED BY BISHOPS, PRIESTS AND DEACONS IN WORSHIP.

What color vestments are being used in church this week?

_____

What liturgical season is it now?

LITURGICAL MEANS HOW WE PRAY AND CELEBRATE AS A CHURCH.

_____

Liturgical colors

White reminds us of purity, joy, and truth. We use it on the Sundays of Christmas and Easter.

Red reminds us of fire and blood. We use it on Pentecost. We might also use it on Palm Sunday and Good Friday.

Green reminds us of God's creation. We use it on Sundays after Epiphany and Pentecost.

Violet reminds us of penitence. We use it on Sundays during Advent and Lent.

PENITENCE MEANS BEING SORRY.

Some churches use different colors. They might use blue, a color of day time and of Mary, during Advent. They might use black, a color of sadness, on Good Friday. They might use rose, a color of joy, for the third Sunday in Advent and the fourth Sunday of Lent.

We dress up the altar and the clergy with these colors to show that the Eucharist is a liturgical celebration. That means we celebrate with the whole Church, throughout the whole year.

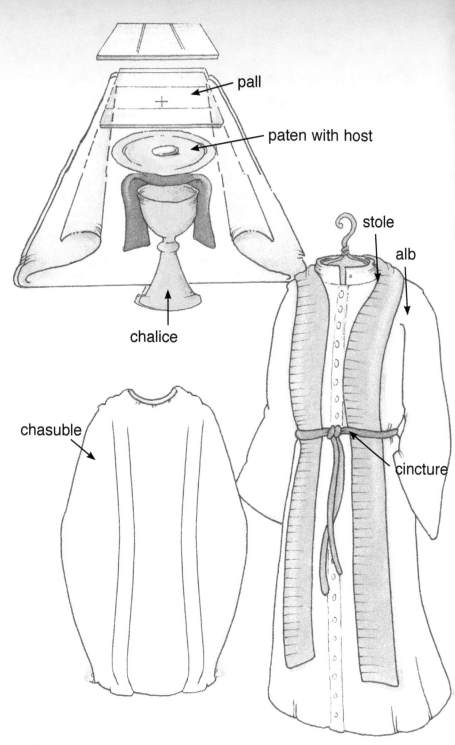

pall

paten with host

stole

alb

chalice

chasuble

cincture

We call the Eucharist a sacrament. A sacrament is a mystery. It has an outside that we can see and touch and hear. The mystery is that a sacrament has an inside, too. We cannot see the inside of a sacrament, but God uses the inside of a sacrament to give us grace.

The "outward and visible" signs of the Eucharist—the things we can see and touch—are the bread and wine. God's work and human hands together make wheat and grapes into bread and wine.

The "inward and spiritual grace" of the Eucharist is that these ordinary things become the body and blood of Christ, our "holy food and drink." They join us to Jesus and to each other.

Earlier you drew a picture of Communion bread. Now draw a picture of a chalice filled with Communion wine.

A CHALICE IS A CUP.

4 Praying Together:
The Shape of the Eucharist

The Word of God

Different churches use different forms to celebrate the Holy Eucharist, but each form follows a pattern. Usually we begin with a hymn, a song to God. The very first prayer is called a "collect" because it collects or gathers the people from whatever else they might be thinking about. Collects always begin by calling on God. The Collect for Purity at the beginning of the Eucharist calls God "Almighty." What are some other ways that people name God?

A collect then asks God to do something for us. **The Collect for Purity** asks God to help us be ready for worship. What else would you like to ask God to do?

A collect ends in the Name of Jesus, such as: "through Jesus Christ our Lord. Amen."

After this opening collect, we sing or say a **hymn of praise**, and then the priest prays a special collect just for that day. When the prayer is over, we sit down to listen to

readings from the Bible. We stand up again to hear the **Gospel**, because that's the story about Jesus. Draw a picture of your favorite story about Jesus.

What do you like best about that story?

After the gospel reading, we sit down to listen to the **sermon.** The priest or deacon helps explain how Jesus' story connects to our lives now.

When the sermon is over, we stand up to say the **Nicene Creed**, which begins "We believe..." It names our belief in God the Father and Creator; in Jesus, God's Son, our Savior and companion; and in the Holy Spirit who lives in our hearts and speaks through the prophets.

Then we **pray for people and places** around the world. First, we **pray for the Church.** Your own part of the worldwide Church is your parish. Draw a picture of where your parish gathers to pray.

We pray for peace throughout the world. Draw a picture of peace.

We pray for people who are sick or sad. Draw a picture of a person who needs our prayers.

We pray for those who have died. Who are some people you would like to pray for that are sick or lonely or sad, or who have died? Are there other people or places you want to pray for?

When we finish praying for others, we kneel down and **ask God to forgive us** for the wrong things we have done, and for not doing things we should have done. We ask God to help us do better. The priest then tells us that God loves and forgives us and will be with us to help us do the right thing.

Once we have been forgiven, we stand up and exchange **The Peace of the Lord**. We greet one another and say, "The peace of the Lord be always with you." We share the peace with those around us in church, thinking also of all the other people we know. We wish God's peace for them, too.

Draw a picture of people exchanging the Peace.

The Holy Communion

Once we begin sharing the Peace, the service moves from words to actions. Next comes the **offertory**, where the bread and wine for Communion are brought to the altar. We also offer gifts of money to show our thanks to God. In our hearts, we offer all our gifts to God. What gifts do you bring to God? What are some things that you are especially thankful for in your life?

Next comes the **Great Thanksgiving.** This is a long prayer. First we join each other and the "Angels and Archangels and all the company of heaven" in offering praise to God.

Draw your idea of what angels
praising God might look like.

Imagine that angels are right there with you when you sing or say:

> Holy, Holy, Holy Lord, God of power and
>   might,
> heaven and earth are full of your glory.
> Hosanna in the highest.
> Blessed is he who comes in the name of
>   the Lord.
> Hosanna in the highest.

In the **prayer of consecration** that follows we hear stories about our past, especially about Jesus. We hear about the Last Supper where Jesus blessed the bread and wine and told his friends—and us—"Do this in remembrance of me." The priest asks the Holy Spirit to make the bread and wine into "holy food and drink" for us, and to make us holy people. We end this prayer with a loud **AMEN!** The word "amen" means "may it be so." It means that you agree with what has just been said by the priest.

Write the word Amen in loud, giant letters below. Draw the loudest Amen that you can!

Whenever you say "Amen," you are saying, "Yes! I agree! That's right and true!"

Next we all pray the **Lord's Prayer** together:

Our Father, who art in heaven,	Our Father in heaven
hallowed be thy Name,	hallowed be your Name,
thy kingdom come,	your kingdom come,
thy will be done,	your will be done,
on earth as it is in heaven.	on earth as in heaven.
Give us this day our daily bread.	Give us today our daily bread.
And forgive us our trespasses,	Forgive us our sins
as we forgive those	as we forgive those
who trespass against us.	who sin against us.
And lead us not into temptation,	Save us from the time of trial,
but deliver us from evil	and deliver us from evil.
For thine is the kingdom,	For the kingdom, the power
and the power, and the glory	and the glory are yours
for ever and ever. Amen.	now and for ever. Amen.

This is a prayer that Jesus taught his disciples, and he wants us to know it, too.

Then, at last, comes the most special and holy part of the service, the part everything else has gotten us ready for: **Holy Communion**. Each time you lift up your hands for the bread and wine, you are united with Jesus. It's as though you are there at the Last Supper with Jesus and he is welcoming you into his family.

Draw a picture of you receiving Communion.

Once everyone has taken Communion, we offer a prayer of thanksgiving to God for "feeding us with spiritual food" and uniting us with Jesus. We also ask for help in living good lives during the week ahead.

Then the priest blesses us. Sometimes we sing a closing hymn. At the very end of the service the deacon or priest dismisses us. They might say, "Let us go forth in the name of Christ." We answer: "Thanks be to God."

Draw the door you go out of as you leave church. Know that Jesus goes with you out that door and into the rest of your life.

5 Manners and Customs:
The Body Language of Prayer

We pray many ways.

Sometimes we stand up and sing to God.
Draw a picture of someone singing to God.

Sometimes we kneel and bow our heads in prayer. Draw a picture of someone kneeling in prayer.

Sometimes we sit and listen prayerfully to readings from the Bible. Draw a picture of someone listening quietly.

Sometimes we stand and pray out loud.
Sometimes we sit silently and just rest in God.
No matter how we pray, God hears all our
prayers, even the silent ones.

(**Note**: Many people like to come a few
minutes early to church so they can have
some quiet prayer time before the service. It's
always good to honor their quiet time with our
own silence.)

In different churches, people use their bodies differently for prayer.

- Some will face the altar and kneel or bow before entering or leaving their seat.

- Some will make the sign of the cross at the end of the creed or before receiving Communion. This is an ancient gesture that honors the presence of Christ.

- When the deacon or priest introduces the Gospel reading, some people use their right thumb to make a cross on their foreheads, lips, and hearts. They invite Christ into their thinking (forehead), speaking (lips), and feeling (heart).

- Some stand as children of God to receive Communion. This is what people did in the early church and is still the custom in Eastern Orthodox tradition.

- Some kneel for Communion as a sign of humble gratitude for God's gifts.

- We lift our hands out or up to receive Communion, often resting the right hand on top of the left, opening our hands to receive Jesus' generous gift of himself.

Draw a pair of hands reaching out to receive Communion.

All these different postures and movements are meant to help us worship God with our whole bodies, not just with our hearts and minds. You probably already know what the customs are at your own church, but when you visit other churches you might see different ways of praying. God hears all prayers.

Sometimes people call the church building "God's House," but remember that God is always with you, wherever you go and whatever you do. God doesn't just live in the church. What the building provides is a holy place, a place apart. In this building we can give our attention to God, listen to stories about God, and join together with Jesus and with each other and with all Christians—even with all the angels and archangels and all those who have gone before us.

Draw a picture of yourself surrounded by your family and by Jesus and by angels.

The Eucharist enfolds us all in God's tender care, and then sends us out to be holy people in the world. It is Jesus' gift to us.

Thanks be to God!